AS THE POET PUT IT, "ONLY GOD CAN MAKE A TREE", BUT YA'AKOV KIRSCHEN HAS GONE HIM ONE BETTER. HE HAS MADE A BOOK ABOUT A TREE ABOUT THE JEWS ABOUT THE WORLD ABOUT IT ALL ABOUT A TREE. ON THE SEVENTH DAY, I ASSUME, YA'AKOV WILL REST.

- JULES FEIFFER

With thanks to the many people who
helped ... but especially to Stuart Paskow
who made it happen ... and to Sally Ariel,
for art direction, editing, coloring the
cover, and damage control.

TREES

...THE GREEN TESTAMENT

BY *Kirschen*.

VITAL MEDIA ENTERPRISES

Trees . . . The Green Testament

and its entire contents ©1993 Ya'akov Kirschen

Library of Congress Catalog Card Number:
93-61529

First Edition First Printing

Published by
Vital Media Enterprises
80 Eighth Avenue
New York, NY 10011

Printed on recycled paper

This book is dedicated to the generation that tried to sing its song to us... and to the generation to which we now attempt to sing.

CONTENTS

9

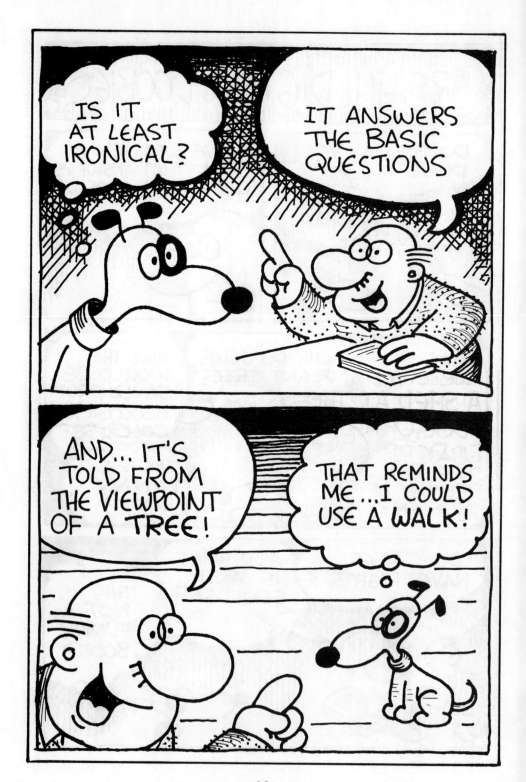

CHAPTER ONE

HE WAS A CRAZY OLD MAN ... THE KIND THAT TALKS TO PLANTS

AND **WE**? ... WE WERE SAPLINGS, YOUNG, TENDER, AND STILL IN OUR POTS.

THOSE WERE THE DAYS WHEN WE THOUGHT WE KNEW EVERYTHING

...WHEN WE WERE THE BIGGEST, GRANDEST, **OLDEST** TREES WE HAD **EVER** SEEN!

TWO LONG YEARS HAD PASSED SINCE THE DAY THAT WE PUSHED OUR FIRST LEAVES OUT OF THE MOIST SOIL OF OUR SPROUTING TRAY IN THE HALL OF GENERATIONS.

...WHERE YOUNG SPROUTS FIRST BLINK INTO CONSCIOUSNESS

...WHERE EACH NEW LIFE IS DROPPED INTO ITS VERY OWN CONTAINER

AND MOVED TO THE WARM ROOM...

...WHERE OUR ROOTS BEGIN TO GROW

AND THEN, WE
ARE MOVED AGAIN!

OUR PLASTIC POTS
ARE CLICKED
TOGETHER IN
A FRAME...

CLICK

...SIX OF US
IN A ROW

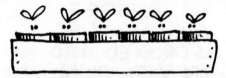

...SIX ROWS
IN A FRAME

THIRTY SIX
FRAMES
IN A LINE...

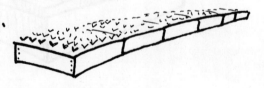

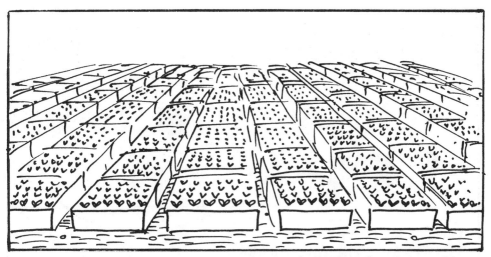

AND LINES OF FRAMES AS FAR AS A SPROUT COULD SEE...

HIGH ABOVE US HANGS THE CANOPY WHICH PROTECTS US FROM THE STRANGE WINGED CREATURES WHICH FLIT AND DART IN THE MYSTERIOUS REGION BEYOND THE NET.

21

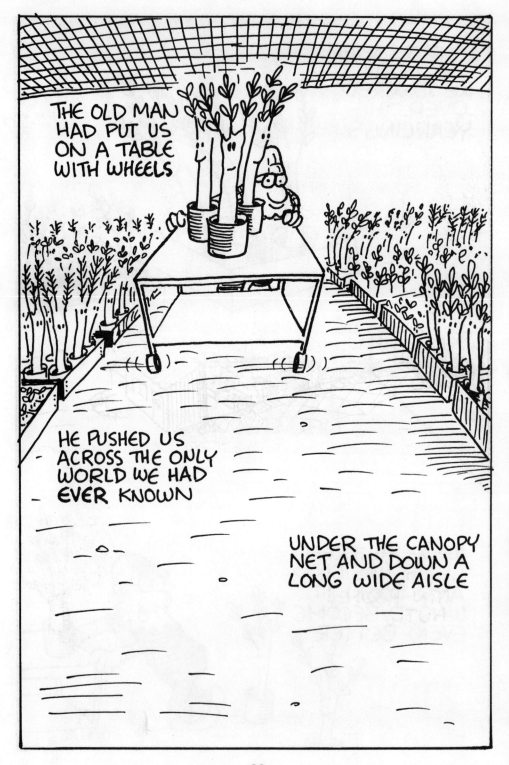

AND CARRIED
US INTO THIS
TIN-ROOFED
HUT...

...A SHED
AT THE EDGE
OF A FOREST

24

HE RAMBLED **ON AND ON** ABOUT THE WORLD "OUTSIDE"

ABOUT HIS PEOPLE ...AND HOW THE NATIONS OF THE WORLD HAD TRIED TO "DESTROY" THEM

AND HOW THEY HAD RETURNED TO THIS, THE LAND FROM WHICH THEY HAD BEEN UPROOTED...

AND HOW THEY WERE BRINGING THE LAND BACK TO LIFE... PLANT BY PLANT, BUSH BY BUSH, TREE BY TREE.

BUT, LIKE I SAID, HE WAS A **CRAZY OLD MAN!**

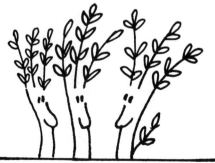

...THE KIND THAT TALKS TO **PLANTS!!**

HE WATERED US AND HE CHATTED WITH US...

...WE WERE HAPPY AND COMFORTABLE IN THE SHED

AND THEN, ONE DAY HE TOOK US...
...OUTSIDE ?!!

"OUTSIDE"?!

THERE WAS **NO** CANOPY NET OR HUT ROOF OVER OUR HEADS TO PROTECT US !?!

THIS "OUTSIDE" SEEMED TO BE EVEN BIGGER THAN THE SHED WORLD!

IT FELT AS IF WE WERE BEING WATCHED!!

...BUT WHO COULD BE WATCHING US?!!

28

29

CHAPTER TWO

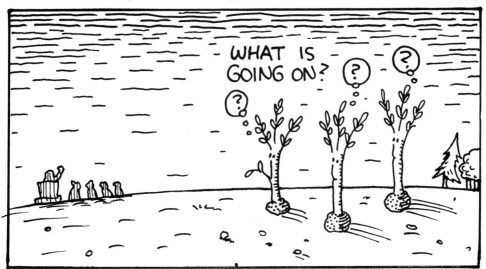

34

AND AFTER THEY LEAVE...

THE OLD MAN WATERS EACH AND EVERY ONE OF US...

AND HE SMILES AND SAYS...

TASTE THE SOIL OF YOUR HOMELAND, MY CHILDREN

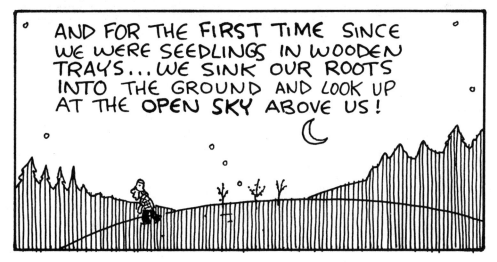

AND FOR THE FIRST TIME SINCE WE WERE SEEDLINGS IN WOODEN TRAYS...WE SINK OUR ROOTS INTO THE GROUND AND LOOK UP AT THE OPEN SKY ABOVE US!

THE NEWLY PLANTED SAPLINGS ARE, AT FIRST, CONFUSED AND FRIGHTENED BY THE INCREDIBLE DIN OF WHAT SEEMS TO BE AN ARGUMENT BETWEEN EVERY TREE IN THE COUNTRY !?!

THE ARGUMENT IS A DISPUTE ABOUT WHAT TO TELL THE SAPLINGS!

... WE WILL START
WITH THE LONG AGO
TIME CALLED...
IN THE BEGINNING

AND THE NEWLY PLANTED SAPLINGS STRETCH THEIR ROOTS TO HEAR...

...THE OLIVE TREE RETELL THE ANCIENT TALE OF THE START OF THINGS...

CHAPTER THREE

AND THERE
WAS ORDER
AND BALANCE
AND BEAUTY
AND PEACE

...AND IT
WAS GOOD

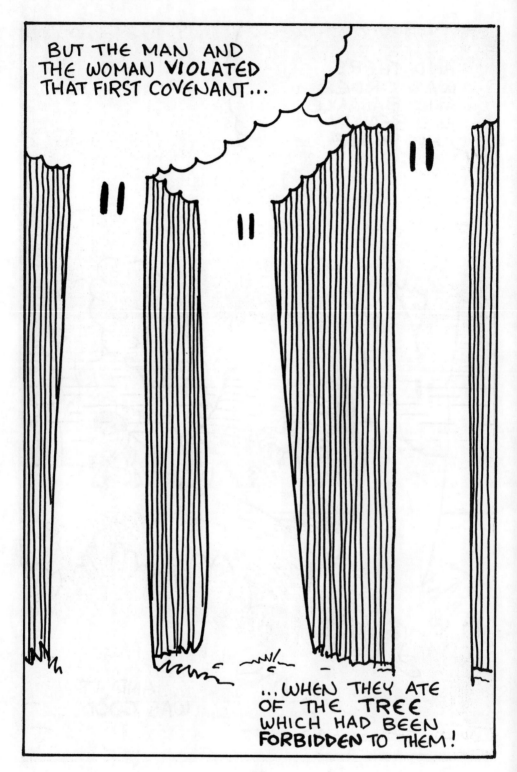

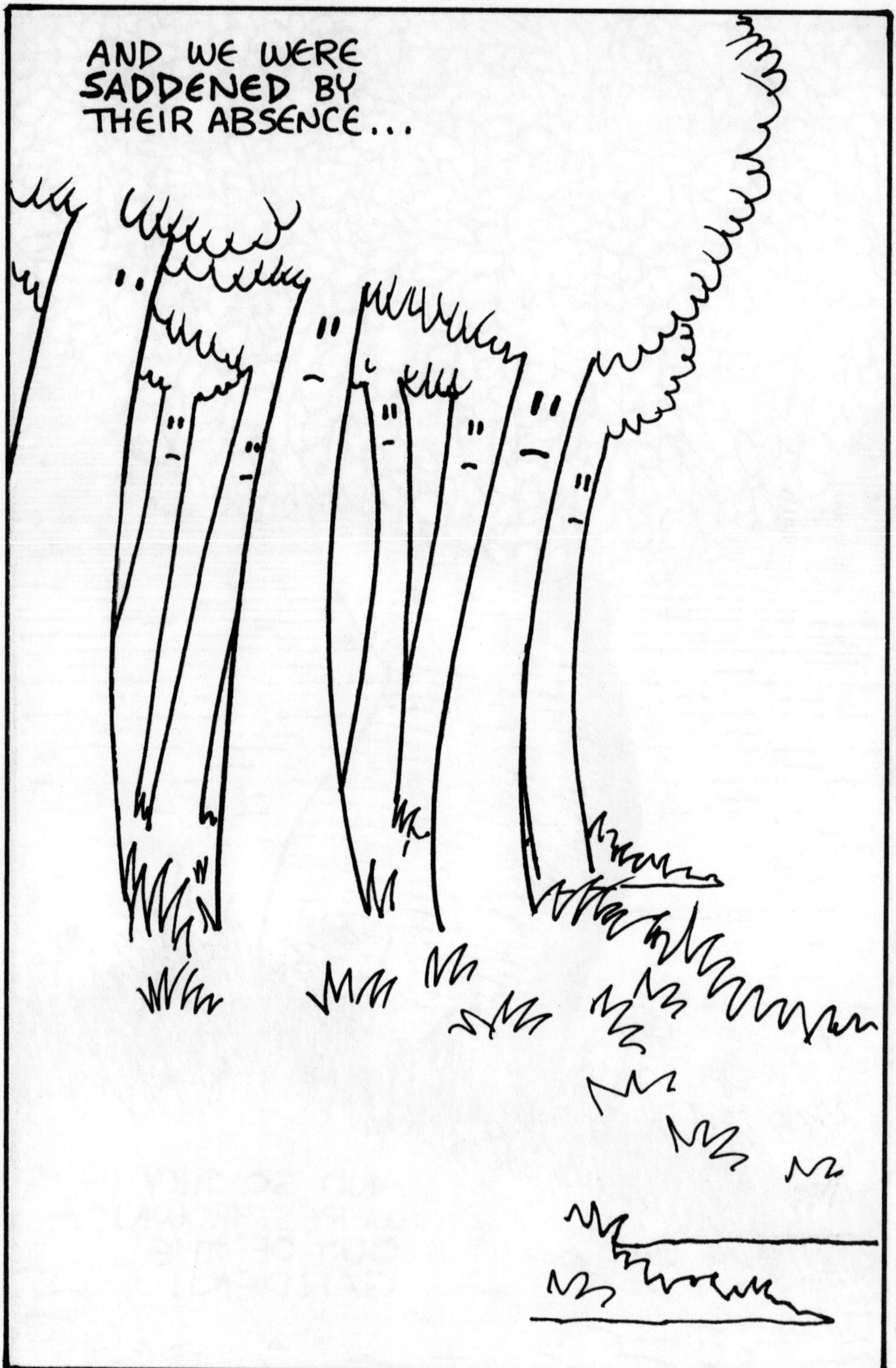
AND WE WERE SADDENED BY THEIR ABSENCE...

... BUT THEY
WERE NOT
READY FOR
PARTNERSHIP!

...WHEN THE FIRST THING MAN **DID** WAS TO BEAT HIS PLOWSHARE INTO A **SWORD**

AND HIS PRUNING HOOK INTO A **SPEAR**

AND HE BEGAN TO **STUDY** THE WAY TO GET WHAT HE **THOUGHT** HE WANTED

SHARPENING AND HONING AN "ARTFORM" WHICH HE DIGNIFIED WITH A NAME OF HIS OWN INVENTION...

WAR

AND **BECAUSE** THEY WERE WITHOUT ROOTS...

.. THEY WERE **NOT** FIXED TO THE EARTH !

... THEY MOVED AND TUMBLED FROM ONE PLACE TO ANOTHER...

LIKE **DEAD LEAVES** AND **DRIED TWIGS** THEY WERE **BLOWN** BY THE WIND. ...**DRIVEN BY INVISIBLE FORCES!**

...THEY MOVED!

THEY HAD BEEN CREATED
TO BE OUR GARDENERS
... BUT THEY HAD BECOME
OUR TORMENTORS

AND WE CRIED OUT
FOR AN END TO
OUR SUFFERING.

AND THEN
FROM OUT
OF THE
DESERT...

AS IF IN
ANSWER
TO OUR
PRAYERS...

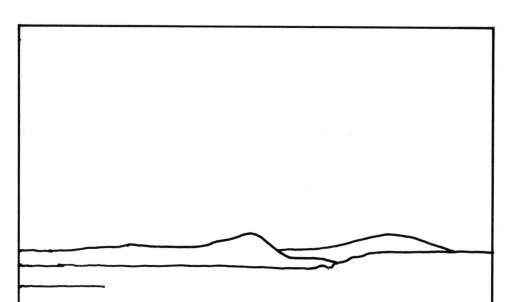

...CAME A PEOPLE CHOSEN TO LIVE IN THIS LAND.

THEY CARRIED WITH THEM A SEVEN-BRANCHED TREE MADE OF GOLD..

AND THEY CARRIED WITH THEM "THE COVENANT"

THE LAND
OPENED
TO THEM.

CHAPTER FOUR

72

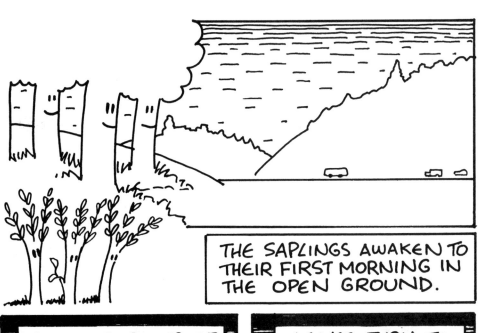

THE SAPLINGS AWAKEN TO THEIR FIRST MORNING IN THE OPEN GROUND.

COOL DROPLETS OF MORNING DEW COVER EACH FINGER OF GRASS

LEAVES TURN TO CATCH AND TASTE THE DELICIOUS FIRST RAYS OF SUNLIGHT.

AND THE ANCIENT TALES OF THE TREES SEEM DISTANT...

...LIKE A DREAM ABOUT TO BE FORGOTTEN?

75

TIME SENSE

THE SHADOWS
GROW LONGER

AND AS THE SAPLINGS
LICK THE LAST DROPS
OF SUNLIGHT...

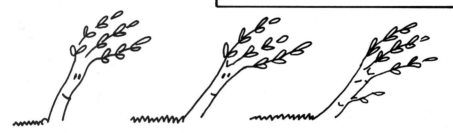

THEIR THOUGHTS RETURN
TO THE STRANGE TALES
OF THE TREES...

AND THEN...
SUDDENLY
IT IS...

SUNSET...

AND THE SAPLINGS STRETCH
THEIR ROOTS TO CATCH THE
VOICES OF THE TREES.

THE LAW PROCLAIMED THE **SPECIALNESS** OF THE TREES

UNTIL A TREE IS OLDER THAN THREE YEARS, ITS FRUIT IS FORBIDDEN TO YOU!

THE LAW PROCLAIMED THE **RIGHTS** OF THE TREES

THOUGH YOU "OWN" AN ORCHARD YOU MAY NOT DENY THE TREE'S RIGHT TO OFFER ITS FRUIT TO A HUNGRY TRAVELER OR WORKER!

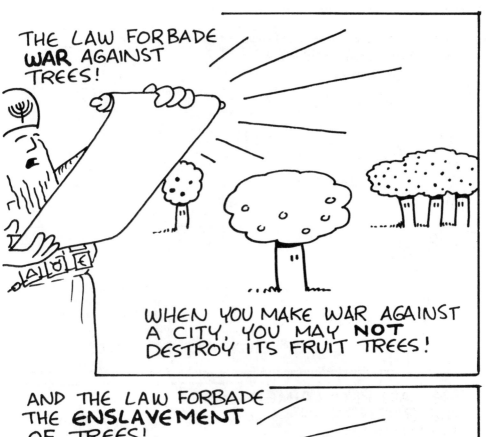

CHAPTER FIVE

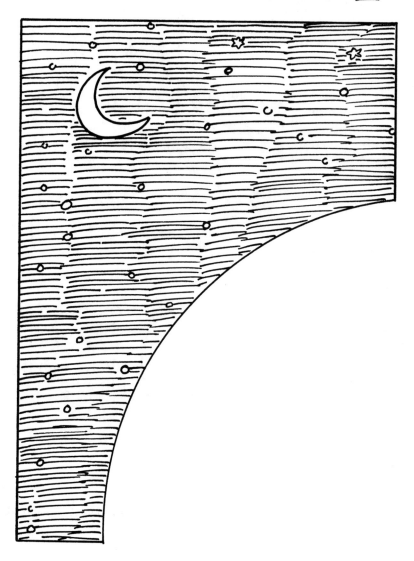

AND THE TATTERED REMNANTS OF THE PROUD
DESERT PEOPLE WERE CARRIED OFF IN CHAINS

UPROOTED FROM THE LAND

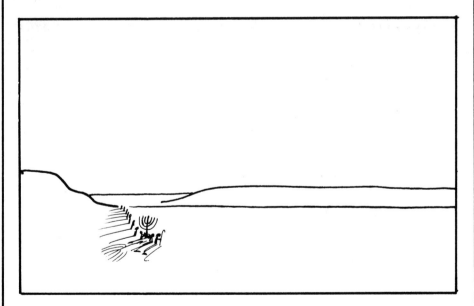

THIRTEEN CENTURIES AFTER THEY HAD
MARCHED IN... WITH A COVENANT IN
THEIR HANDS.

THEY HAD BECOME A NATION WHEN GOD SPOKE TO THEIR PROPHET.... FROM A **TREE** THAT BURNED WITH LIGHT

THEY HAD BECOME A NATION WHEN THEY ACCEPTED THE **COVENANT**

AND WHEN THE "MIGHTIEST" EMPIRE ON EARTH **RIPPED** THEM OUT OF THEIR LITTLE LAND... A TRIUMPHAL ARCH WAS BUILT IN ROME... THE "MIGHTIEST" CITY ON EARTH...

...TO PROUDLY SHOW THE NATIONS OF MAN THAT THEY HAD CRUSHED THE PEOPLE OF THE COVENANT AND CARRIED OFF THE TREE OF GOLD

THE DARKNESS OF NIGHT BEGINS TO RETREAT...

THE TREES TURN THEIR LEAVES TO FACE THE SUN OF THE NEW DAY...

THEY TURN FROM THE NIGHT SONG OF TREEDOM...

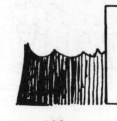

...AND THEIR VOICES FALL STILL.

A TRUCK BACKS CAREFULLY ACROSS THE ROCKY GROUND.

THIS IS THE **FIRST** TIME THAT THE SAPLINGS SEE ONE UP CLOSE!

WHAT **WERE** THESE SMOKE-BELCHING MONSTERS THEY'D SEEN ROARING UP AND DOWN ON THE DISTANT ROAD?

AT NIGHT, THEIR EYES SHINING WITH BRIGHT BEAMS OF LIGHT!?

SOON THE ROOTLESS ONES BEGAN TO RELOAD THE BACK OF THEIR GENTLE TRUCK-CREATURE

WITH YOUNGSTERS STILL IN THEIR POTS, FRESH FROM THE POTTING SHED

AND AFTER THE TRUCK-CREATURE HAD CAREFULLY ROLLED OUT OF SIGHT...

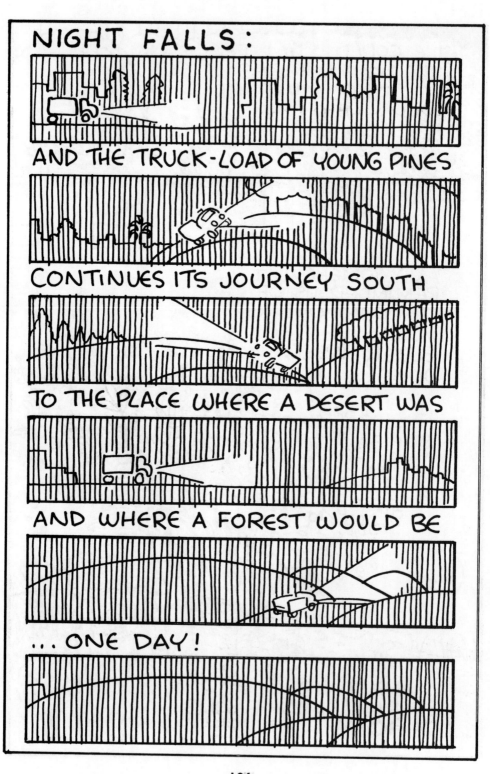

NIGHT FALLS:

AND THE TRUCK-LOAD OF YOUNG PINES

CONTINUES ITS JOURNEY SOUTH

TO THE PLACE WHERE A DESERT WAS

AND WHERE A FOREST WOULD BE

...ONE DAY!

THE STARS ABOVE
US GLOW WITH A
COLD CLARITY...

AS WE BEGIN TO HEAR
THE SONG OF THE ELDERS.

THE RETELLING
OF THE AGES OF
HEROISM AND
OF SURVIVING
AGAINST ALL
ODDS...

. THE SONG OF THE SEPARATION!

"AT NIGHT WE'D LISTEN TO THE **FABLES** OF THE SURVIVORS

THE OLD TREES TOLD **TALL TALES** ABOUT HOW THESE ROOTLESS ONES WITH THEIR KILLING WAYS...

WERE **NOT** THE SONS OF THIS LAND

THE OLD TREES TOLD US **MYTHS** ABOUT A GARDEN AT THE START OF TIME

BUT OUR "MEMORIES" OF THE PAST GREW DIM...

FOR MANY OF US THE ANCIENT PROMISES HAD BECOME JUST A "BEAUTIFUL DREAM"

OUR FAITH IN THE FUTURE BEGAN TO FADE...

...UNTIL ALMOST ALL THAT WAS LEFT WAS THE YEARLY NIGHT OF THE PLEDGE...

...WHEN ALL OF TREEDOM WOULD LINK ROOTS AND RECITE THE ANCIENT CHANT...

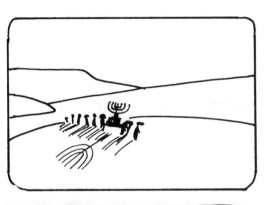

...THE NIGHT WHEN ALL OF TREEDOM WOULD REPEAT THE CALL FOR OUR ANCIENT PEOPLE TO RETURN TO THIS LAND.

STORIES OF WHAT LIFE WOULD BE LIKE IN THE END OF DAYS...

STORIES OF WONDER AND MAGIC AND MIRACLES AND JOY...

STORIES THAT EVEN THE ELDERS THEMSELVES HAD CEASED TO BELIEVE.

AND SO WE LIVED
OUR BRITTLE LIVES

AND WE DIED
OUR COUNTLESS
DEATHS

AND WE WATCHED THE MAN-MADE DESERT
SLOWLY ROLL ACROSS THE LAND...

...LIKE A SPREADING STAIN OF EVIL!

IT IS THE FIRST LIGHT OF DAY

THE YOUNG SAPLINGS STILL TREMBLE WITH THE MEMORY OF THE ROOTLESS ONES AND THEIR TERRIBLE TREE-KILLING WAYS.

THE WARMTH OF THE SUNLIGHT DOES NOT EASE THE CHILL OF FEAR THAT GRIPS THEM

AS THEY THINK OF THE DESERT THAT FOLLOWS THE SPREAD OF MANKIND

...BUT BY SUNSET THEIR THOUGHTS TURN TO THE FATE OF THE PEOPLE OF THE COVENANT WHO HAD BEEN UPROOTED AND CARRIED OFF INTO EXILE.

AND IN THE DARK WINTERS OF EXILE

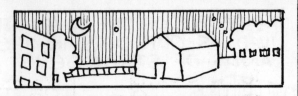

THEY LIT TREE-SHAPED CANDELABRAS...

AND CELEBRATED THEIR REMEMBRANCE OF FREEDOM...

IN THE LAND OF THE COVENANT

SO FAR AWAY THAT IT SOUNDED LIKE A FAIRY TALE FOR CHILDREN

OR A FAINTLY REMEMBERED DREAM.

THEY TOILED AT WHATEVER TASKS WERE NOT FORBIDDEN TO THEM

AND THEIR CHILDREN LEARNED THE CUSTOMS OF THE PLACE

...THEY STUDIED AND THEY EDUCATED THEMSELVES

AND THEY BECAME LIKE THE PEOPLE OF THAT PLACE

THEY LEARNED TO SPEAK THE LANGUAGE OF THAT PLACE

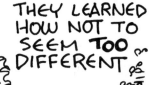

THEY LEARNED HOW NOT TO SEEM **TOO** DIFFERENT

THEY LEARNED TO "FIT IN"

...BUT THEY WOULD **NOT** ACCEPT THE ALIEN GODS

AND THEY WOULD **NOT** GIVE UP THEIR COVENANT.

125

BUT THE OTHER ROOTLESS ONES ALSO THIRSTED FOR THE PROMISE OF PEACE...

...WHICH THEY FOUND IN THE SCROLLS OF THE COVENANT OF THE PEOPLE WHO HAD BEEN CHOSEN.

AND SO THESE OTHER ROOTLESS COPIED THE ANCIENT WORDS INTO OTHER TONGUES...

AND REPRINTED ITS TRANSLATIONS INTO EVERY LANGUAGE SPOKEN BY MANKIND

WHEREVER THERE WERE BOOKS TO BE READ...

...AMONG THEM WAS THE BOOK OF PROMISE, THE BOOK OF THE COVENANT!

ANY MANY WERE THE ROOTLESS WHO READ AND UNDERSTOOD THE MESSAGE OF HOPE

BUT MOST WERE STILL NOT READY FOR PARTNERSHIP

AND THE PEOPLE OF
THE COVENANT WERE
HOUNDED AND MOCKED
AND DRIVEN TO THE
FOUR CORNERS OF
THE EARTH.

AND SO PASSED **NINETEEN CENTURIES** OF SEPARATION

WHILE CONTROL OF THIS TATTERED LITTLE LAND PASSED BACK AND FORTH **FOURTEEN TIMES** BETWEEN INVADERS FROM THE THREE CONTINENTS

LIKE A BONE FOUGHT OVER BY WILD DOGS

AND WE TREES WERE SLAUGHTERED ...AND THE LAND WAS MADE DRY AND PITIFUL...

AND AFTER **NINETEEN** CENTURIES OF SEPARATION...

THE PEOPLE OF THE COVENANT HELD A MEETING ...AND THEY DEVISED...

...A **PLAN!**

THIS LAND THAT WAS DESOLATE BECAME LIKE THE GARDEN

THE RUINED CITIES WERE REBUILT. AND PEOPLE OF THE COVENANT DWELT IN THEM

...AND SO DID WE!

PEOPLE OF THE COVENANT WENT OUT ONTO THE SAND DUNES AT THE EDGE OF THE SEA...

...WHERE THEY BUILT A **NEW** CITY... AND THEY CALLED IT THE CITY OF **ANCIENT SPRING TIME**

AND THE NEW CITY CALLED ANCIENT SPRING TIME PROSPERED... ...AND IT **GREW**

...AND IT BLOSSOMED WITH **EVERY** KIND OF TREE.

135

WE FORESTS
BEGAN TO
RISE AGAIN.

BUT ACROSS THE
REST OF THE PLANET
THE ROOTLESS ONES
MEASURED "PROGRESS"
BY THE NUMBER OF
ACRES OF LAND
THAT THEY HAD
"CLEARED" OF
TREES.

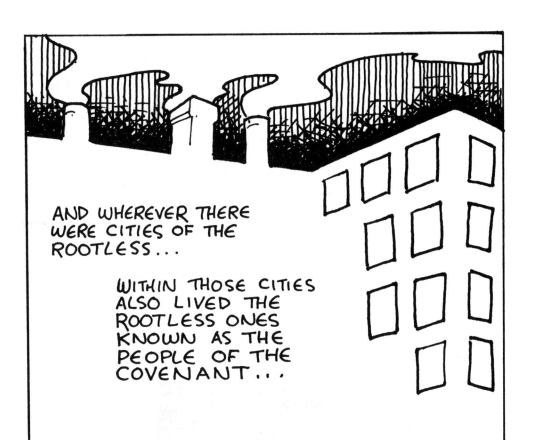

AND WHEREVER THERE
WERE CITIES OF THE
ROOTLESS...

WITHIN THOSE CITIES
ALSO LIVED THE
ROOTLESS ONES
KNOWN AS THE
PEOPLE OF THE
COVENANT...

AND THE WORLD
GREW DARKER

AND EMPIRES
ROSE AND
EMPIRES
FELL!

EACH EMPIRE TRIED TO EXPLAIN THE SUFFERING OF THE ROOTLESS BY...

...REWRITING HISTORY!

THEY WOULD INVENT A **NEW PAST** TO BELIEVE IN.

HEY! THERE'S ONE OF THEM DIRTY @!?#%! COVENANT FOLLOWERS!

144

AND THE PEOPLE OF THE COVENANT WHO HAD SURVIVED IN THE LANDS THAT HAD CURSED THEM

...CAME OUT OF THE WRECKAGE OF THE LANDS OF DESPAIR

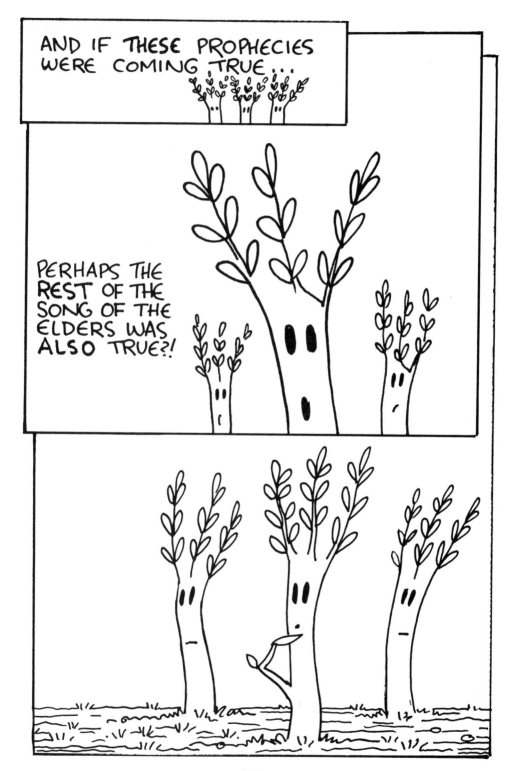

AND IF THESE PROPHECIES WERE COMING TRUE...

PERHAPS THE REST OF THE SONG OF THE ELDERS WAS ALSO TRUE?!

154

...THE GARDENER OF A GARDEN WORLD.

CHAPTER SIX

THE RAINS OF WINTER POUND THE FOREST...

...BUT THE DOWNPOUR HITS THE UMBRELLA OF TREE TOPS

AND THE DROPS OF WATER FALL **GENTLY** TO THE FOREST FLOOR BELOW

WHERE THE ROOTS OF THE TREES HOLD THE EARTH

AND THE TOP SOIL IS **NOT** WASHED AWAY...

AND EVEN THE YOUNGEST SAPLINGS
DO THEIR SHARE OF THE WORK
... AND THEY ARE **PROUD**

164

COMING OF AGE

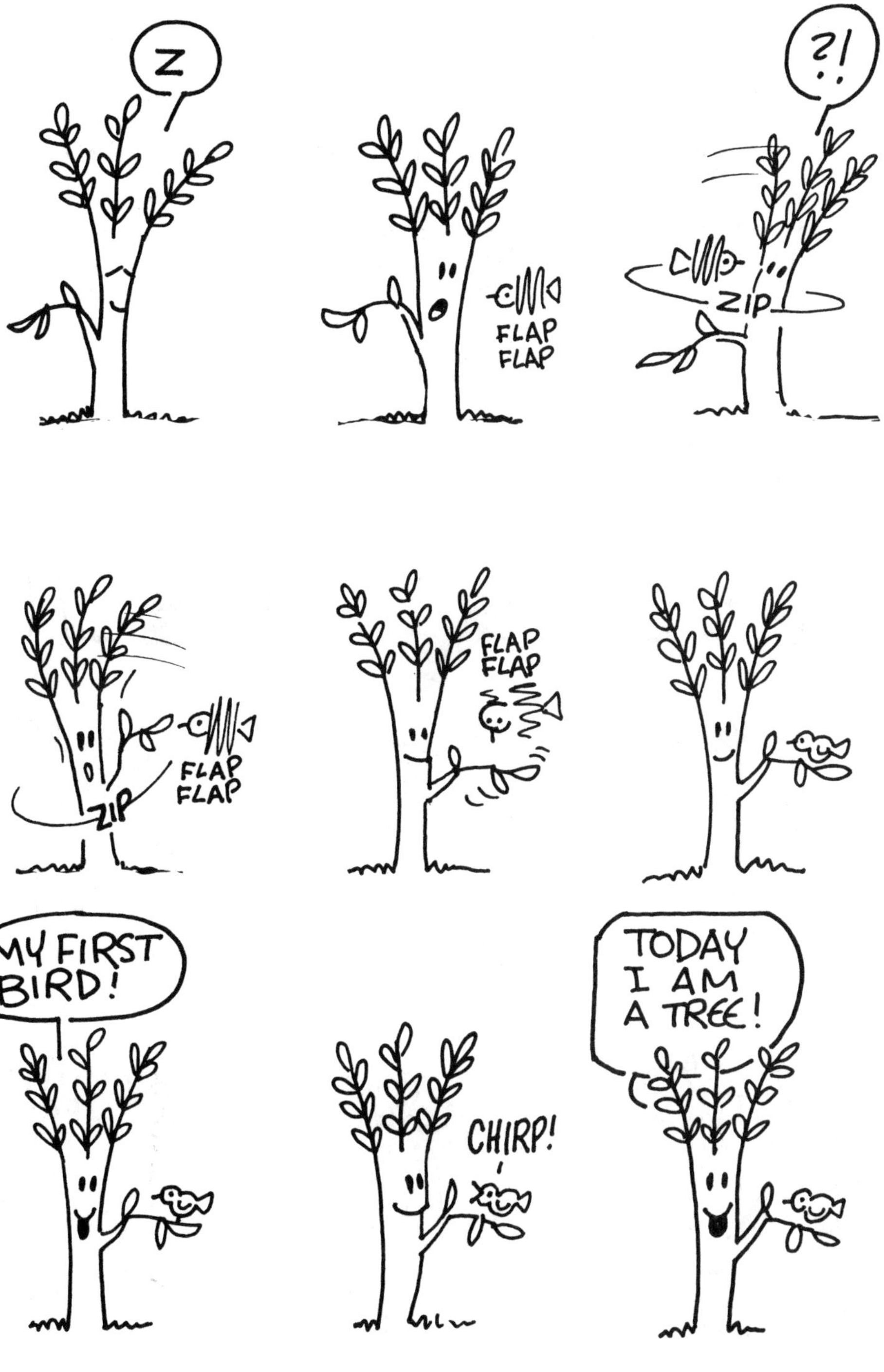

166

IT IS THE SOUND OF CHILDREN. CHILDREN? HERE IN THE FOREST?!

AND THEY SPOKE OF HOW, IN THE WAKE OF THE HORROR... OUT OF THE DEATH AND DESPAIR, SURVIVORS HAD COME HOME TO THE LAND OF THE COVENANT...

THEY TOLD OF HOW THE DRY BONES AND WASTED BODIES OF THEIR PEOPLE HAD BECOME A MIGHTY NATION IN THEIR LAND...

AND THEY TOLD OF HOW THIS FOREST WOULD BE A MEMORIAL TO THE CHILDREN WHO HAD BEEN KILLED...

172

THE SAPLINGS SHAKE THEMSELVES OUT OF THEIR REMEMBERING...

IN TIME TO HEAR THE CHILDREN CLAMOR ABOARD THE BUS.

AND THE JOY OF THEIR SHOUTING AND THE MELODY OF THEIR SINGING

...FADES WITH THE PURR OF THE MOTOR

..AS THE BUS ROLLS OUT OF THE FOREST, CARRYING ITS PRECIOUS CARGO BACK TO THE CITY OF ANCIENT SPRING-TIME

JUST DOWN THE ROAD FROM WHERE PEOPLE OF THE COVENANT DWELT IN THEIR CITY OF PEACE ON THE MOUNTAIN OF THE LORD

AND AROUND WHICH THEY HAD PLANTED FORESTS OF PEACE AND GROVES OF REMEMBRANCE.

EPILOGUE

A CELEBRATION OF THE PEOPLE WHO HAD SURVIVED THEIR LONG MARCH THROUGH TIME...

TODAY, THE RETURN OF THE PEOPLE OF THE COVENANT AND THE REFORESTING OF THE LAND SEEMS **ORDINARY**

BUT THIS "ORDINARY" DAY WILL **ONE** DAY SEEM AS **MIRACULOUS** AS THE GREATEST DAYS OF **PAST** AGES OF **WONDER**...

AND THE SONG OF THE SAPLINGS WILL BLEND WITH THE SONGS OF THE OTHER TREES OF THE LAND

THE TREES ON THE HILLS OVER THE LAKE OF MIRACLES

THE TREES ON THE PLAINS WHERE THE SUN HAD STOOD STILL

THE TREES ON THE SHORES OF THE SEA THAT HAD PARTED

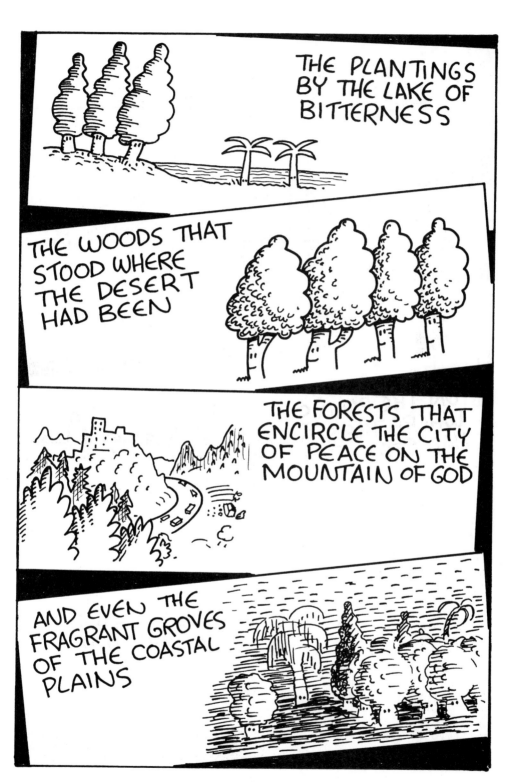

THE PLANTINGS BY THE LAKE OF BITTERNESS

THE WOODS THAT STOOD WHERE THE DESERT HAD BEEN

THE FORESTS THAT ENCIRCLE THE CITY OF PEACE ON THE MOUNTAIN OF GOD

AND EVEN THE FRAGRANT GROVES OF THE COASTAL PLAINS

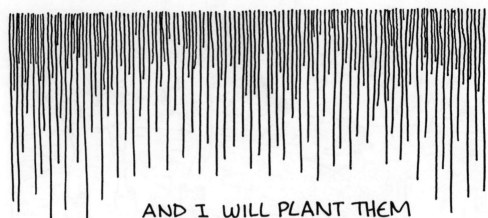

AND I WILL PLANT THEM UPON THEIR LAND, AND THEY SHALL NO MORE BE PULLED UP OUT OF THEIR LAND WHICH I HAVE GIVEN THEM, SAITH THE LORD THY GOD

-AMOS IX:15